THE AMAZING BOOK OF
3-D THRILLERS!
fantastic eye-popping experiences

ARCTURUS

ARCTURUS

This edition published in 2011 by Arcturus Publishing Limited
26/27 Bickels Yard, 151–153 Bermondsey Street,
London SE1 3HA

ISBN: 978-1-84837-876-6
CH001827EN

Authors: Paul Harrison, Heather Amery, Lynn Gibbons,Chris Coode

Supplier 03, Date 0711, Print run 842

Printed in China

CONTENTS

DINOSAURS

Millions and millions of years before any people lived on Earth, the world belonged to the dinosaurs. These amazing creatures first appeared about 228 million years ago. The magnificent beasts ranged in size from the knee-high to the sky-high, and ruled the Earth for about 160 million years. Humans have only been around for about 1.5 million years, so we have quite a lot of catching up to do!

DINOSAUR DAYS

Dinosaurs lived during the Mesozoic Era, which began 245 million years ago and ended 65 million years ago. Each of three periods in the Mesozoic Era had its own cool creatures. The Triassic Period (248–206 million years ago) gave us the earliest dinosaurs, like *Herrerasaurus* (eh-ray-rah-SORE-us), as well as the first small mammals. The Jurassic Period (206–142 million years ago) produced plant-eaters like *Stegosaurus* (steg-oh-SORE-us) and meat-eaters like *Allosaurus* (al-oh-SORE-us). And the Cretaceous Period (142–65 million years ago) was the time of *Iguanodon* (ig-WHA-noh-don) and *Deinonychus* (die-NON-i-kus) and, sadly, the end of the line for the dinosaurs.

◄ EMPTY NESTERS

Like most reptiles, dinosaurs hatched from eggs. For many years, palaeontologists (scientists who study prehistoric life) thought that dinosaurs were pretty relaxed parents: in their tough neighbourhood, self-preservation was a higher priority than taking care of the children! But fossils now indicate that some dinosaurs may have been very protective of their young, like one Cretaceous plant-eater who apparently guarded its babies and brought them food. This dinosaur has been named *Maiasaura* (my-ah-SORE-ah), or 'good mother lizard'.

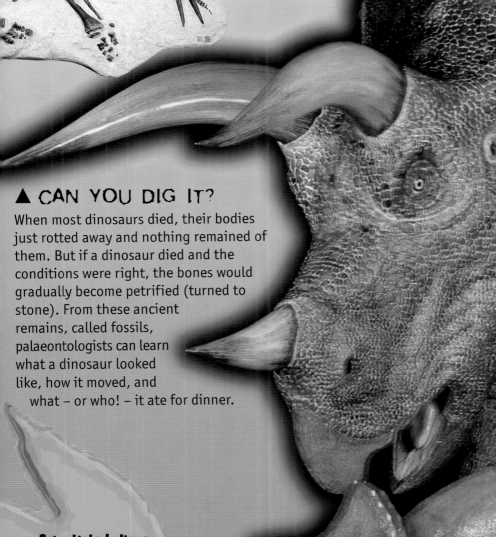

▲ CAN YOU DIG IT?

When most dinosaurs died, their bodies just rotted away and nothing remained of them. But if a dinosaur died and the conditions were right, the bones would gradually become petrified (turned to stone). From these ancient remains, called fossils, palaeontologists can learn what a dinosaur looked like, how it moved, and what – or who! – it ate for dinner.

Scientists believe there are hundreds of dinosaur species yet to be found. You might be the person to make the next big discovery!

Mighty Meat

Carnivorous dinosaurs, the most fearsome of all, would not have won any popularity contests. Some, like the recently discovered *Giganotosaurus* (JI-gah-NO-tuh-SORE-us), were humongous, but there were also mini meat-munchers like *Compsognathus* (komp-soh-NAY-thus), which was no bigger than a modern chicken. But they all had the same favourite food — meat — and the tools to get it with. When their dagger-like flesh-ripping teeth broke or wore out, new ones grew to take their place. No dentures for these dudes!

Palaeontologists can learn what dinosaurs ate by examining fossils called coprolites – the scientific name for dino dung.

◄ RUN FOR YOUR LIFE!

Some of the most dangerous carnivorous dinosaurs were small but speedy – and well-armed! *Deinonychus* was only 3.5 metres (11.5 feet) long, but fast and fierce. Its name, meaning 'terrible claw', refers to the long, curved claw on each of its back feet, which it used to slash its prey. It also had a relatively big brain – bad news for its intended victims.

EATERS

FOOD FIGHTS ▶

While some herbivorous (plant-eating) dinosaurs may have been gentle, they didn't necessarily give up without a struggle. In Mongolia's Gobi Desert, the bones of a meat-eating *Velociraptor* (vel-O-si-RAP-tor, meaning 'speedy robber') and the bones of a plant-eating *Protoceratops* (pro-toe-SER-a-tops) were found together, indicating a fight to the finish – for both of them. So much for fast food!

▼ ARMED AND DANGEROUS

At under 11 metres (36 feet) long, *Allosaurus* was the top predator of the Jurassic Period. It had a powerful tail, three strong claws on each hand, and a mouthful of teeth with jagged edges, perfect for tearing and chewing flesh. You wouldn't hear this diner complain that his meat was too tough!

The great meat-eater *Megalosaurus* (MEG-ah-loh-SORE-us), or 'great reptile', was the first dinosaur ever to be named. When its leg bone was unearthed, people first thought they had discovered the remains of a giant man.

9

Herbivores: g

The biggest creatures ever to walk the Earth were the herbivorous (plant-eating) dinosaurs. Just the neck of the *Mamenchisaurus* (mah-MEN-chee-SORE-us) measured 12 metres (39 feet) — the length of a bus. Another long-neck, *Seismosaurus* (SIZE-moh-sore-us), may have measured nearly 40 metres (131 feet). That's the length of two bowling alley lanes! The plant-eaters went looking for food, not trouble, so other dinosaurs had little to fear from them. But a meat-eater that provoked or attacked them might get more than it bargained for.

▲ VEGETARIAN VENGEANCE

Imagine long-necked reptiles the height of six men standing on each other's shoulders. One of these creatures alone would be as heavy as a dozen elephants! *Brachiosaurus* (brak-ee-oh-SORE-us) was too massive to move fast. But it had a thick and powerful tail, great for whacking Jurassic attackers like *Allosaurus* and *Ceratosaurus* (seh-rat-oh-SORE-us). And while its thick, tree-like limbs weren't built for speed, *Brachiosaurus* might have been able to rear up on its hind legs and crash its front legs down on its enemy. Take that!

◀ TOUGH LOVE

The plant-eating *Pachycephalosaurus* (PAK-ee-SEF-a-loh-SORE-us) was a real bonehead! The solid dome on top of its skull was 25 centimetres (10 inches) thick. Some scientists believe that during the mating season, rival males would fight for females by charging at each other head first. Those built-in crash helmets certainly came in handy!

ENTLE giants?

▼ WEAPONS OR WEATHERPROOFING?

The strange-looking *Stegosaurus* has long puzzled palaeontologists. Most now agree that its triangular plates formed a row down its back and served as a sort of prehistoric furnace *and* air-conditioner. *Stegosaurus* may have turned its plates towards the sun to soak up rays to warm its body, while a breeze through the plates would cool it down. Scientists used to think that the plates discouraged predators from snacking on *Stegosaurus,* but further study has revealed that they weren't really very sturdy. Fortunately, the one-metre-long, spear-like spikes on its tail would have been excellent weapons.

Poor *Stegosaurus* has another claim to fame besides its weird appearance: its walnut-sized brain was smaller than any other dinosaur's.

The polished pebbles found among some plant-eating dinosaur remains suggest that before they gulped down their leafy lunches, some dinosaurs may have swallowed stones to help grind up their food.

Tyrannosauru

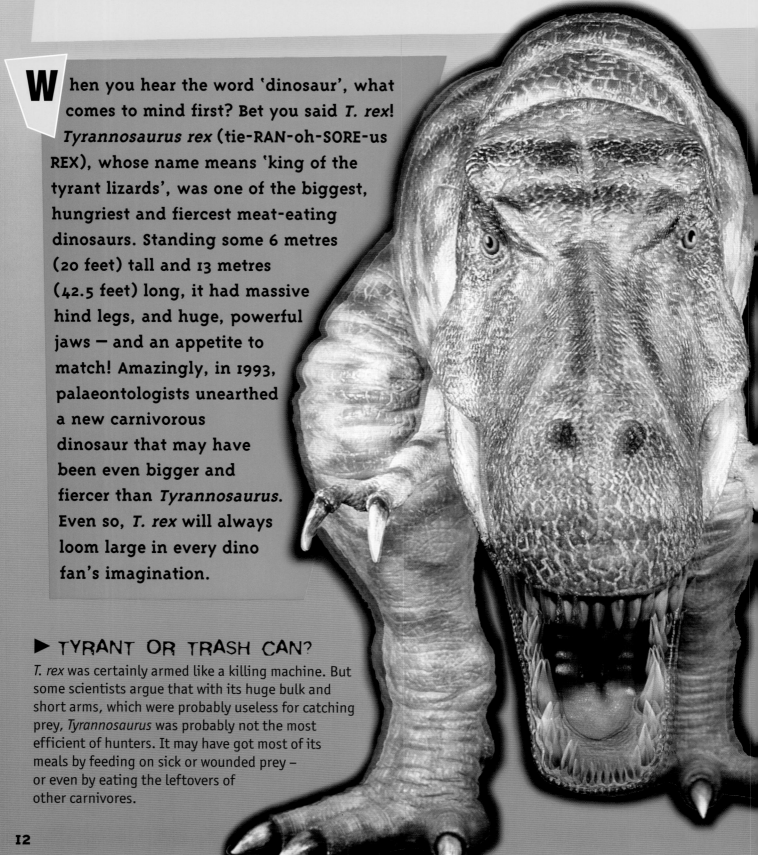

When you hear the word 'dinosaur', what comes to mind first? Bet you said *T. rex*! *Tyrannosaurus rex* (tie-RAN-oh-SORE-us REX), whose name means 'king of the tyrant lizards', was one of the biggest, hungriest and fiercest meat-eating dinosaurs. Standing some 6 metres (20 feet) tall and 13 metres (42.5 feet) long, it had massive hind legs, and huge, powerful jaws — and an appetite to match! Amazingly, in 1993, palaeontologists unearthed a new carnivorous dinosaur that may have been even bigger and fiercer than *Tyrannosaurus*. Even so, *T. rex* will always loom large in every dino fan's imagination.

▶ TYRANT OR TRASH CAN?

T. rex was certainly armed like a killing machine. But some scientists argue that with its huge bulk and short arms, which were probably useless for catching prey, *Tyrannosaurus* was probably not the most efficient of hunters. It may have got most of its meals by feeding on sick or wounded prey — or even by eating the leftovers of other carnivores.

S: THE EX-REX?

T. rex would have needed to eat about 290 teachers a year to satisfy its enormous appetite!

▲ ALL THE BETTER TO EAT YOU WITH

Tyrannosaurus rex was certainly a big-mouth! With a head as long as a refrigerator, it could have opened its jaws wide enough to swallow a man in one gulp. Curved, jagged teeth, longer than a human hand, could puncture its prey's organs before tearing it apart. *T. rex*'s teeth were made for ripping, not chewing, so it had to swallow each mouthful whole. What dreadful table manners!

SUPER REX

In 1990, one of the largest and most complete *Tyrannosaurus* skeletons ever unearthed was found in South Dakota, USA. Named 'Sue', after its discoverer, this fossilized dinosaur was a real tough customer. A number of its bones had been broken but had rehealed over time. The broken bones were probably a result of fierce battles with other *T. rex*.

THE RIGHTFUL KING ▶

Giganotosaurus, whose name means 'giant lizard of the south', was discovered in Argentina in 1993. When it was discovered that this dinosaur's skull and thigh bone were bigger than Sue's, it became clear that *Tyrannosaurus* was *rex* no more! How long will *Giganotosaurus* be number one? Its reign could end at any time, since new types of dinosaurs are being found every year. But until then – Long Live the King!

While dinosaurs roamed the Earth, equally awesome beasts ruled the seas. Many of these oceanic monsters evolved from land reptiles and adapted to life in the water. But though some looked pretty fishy, they were still reptiles, and had to come to the surface to breathe between dives, just like whales and dolphins. The prehistoric sea monsters came in all shapes and sizes. Some had long necks and flippers, while others had long jaws filled with razor-sharp teeth. One of the biggest, *Kronosaurus* (KRON-oh-SORE-us), with its 2.5-metre-long (8-foot-long) head, feasted on prehistoric squid, sharks — and its fellow seafaring reptiles!

Beautifully preserved fossils suggest that ichthyosaurs didn't lay eggs but gave birth to their little ones live in the water.

▼ A SPOT OF FISHING

Ichthyosaurs (IKH-thee-oh-sores), like this 15-metre-long (49-foot) *Shonisaurus* (shon-ee-SORE-us), were the super swimmers of the prehistoric seas. They looked and lived a lot like modern-day dolphins – but they were much, much bigger. With sleek bodies, back fins, and strong tails, ichthyosaurs zipped through the water as fast as 40 kph (25 mph). When their big eyes spotted a tasty meal, their long, tooth-lined jaws would open and – snap! Fish *du jour*!

MONSTERS

◄ MONSTER OR MYTH?

Sea monster sightings have been reported all over the world. The most famous of these creatures is Scotland's 'Nessie', the so-called Loch Ness Monster. Descriptions of Nessie – and a photo that turned out to be a fake – made it sound like a plesiosaur. Few people believe there are any such monsters today . . . but never say never!

DOWN IN THE DEPTHS ►

With their skinny necks and roly-poly bodies, plesiosaurs (PLE-see-oh-sores) may have looked awkward, but thanks to paddle-like flippers that let them twist and turn, they were able to swim at high speeds to catch food with their sharp teeth. To help themselves sink, they sometimes swallowed rocks to act as ballast. Now there's an appetizer that would fill anyone up!

In prehistoric times, reptiles not only ruled the Earth and seas but also filled the skies. The pterosaurs (TEH-ruh-sores), flying reptiles with wings made of skin, fed on creatures from both land and sea. Some were as tiny as a sparrow, but others had a wingspan the size of a small aeroplane's — along with knife-sharp teeth. Look out below!

Quetzalcoatlus (kwet-zal-co-AT-lus) was the largest creature ever to sail the skies. And sail or glide on air currents is what it probably did; its enormous wings may have been too big to flap!

▼ SUPER SCOOPER

Pteranodon (Ter-RAN-oh-don) was one funny-looking fisherman. Its head had a pointy crest and even pointier jaws. *Pteranodon* would skim through the water, scoop up fish and swallow them whole — the same handy method used by pelicans today.

AIR-VOLUTION ▶

Rhamphorynchus (RAM-foh-RING-khus), one of the early pterosaurs, had spiky teeth, great for spearing fish. It also had a long, kite-like tail that may have helped it steer through the skies. Later flying reptiles like *Quetzalcoatlus* looked quite different, with much shorter tails but longer necks.

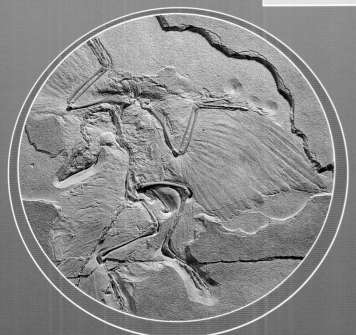

◀ FINALLY...FEATHERS!

Archeopteryx (ark-ee-OP-ter-iks), which means 'ancient wing', is the first flying reptile known to have had feathery wings. But don't let the feathers fool you – this was no ordinary bird. Its fossils reveal the skeleton of a reptile with dinosaur-like teeth and claws on its wings, which it may have used to climb trees. Some scientists think it may have been more of a glider than a flier – okay at catching a breeze, but lousy at take-offs!

The dinosaurs (and their flying and swimming relatives) ruled for 165 million years. But 65 million years ago, they disappeared. What happened? Did something kill them all at once, or did they gradually become extinct over a year . . . a decade . . . a millennium? Did a single catastrophic event kill these creatures, or did a mix of factors cause this disappearing act?

VIOLENT VOLCANOES ▶

One theory blames the dinosaurs' disappearance on huge volcanoes in what is now India. These volcanoes erupted late in the Cretaceous Period, and may have spewed out so much lava, volcanic ash and poisonous gas into the air that it caused the climate to change. The dinosaurs were not able to survive this catastrophe.

ppear

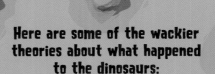

LIGHTS OUT ▶

At the end of the Cretaceous Period, a massive meteorite – more than 10 kilometres (6 miles) wide – may have crashed down on Earth. Many scientists think that the huge clouds of dust from this collision blocked out the sun for weeks, or maybe even months. Plenty of small animals (such as mammals, birds and insects) survived this big bang. However, without sunlight, most plant life died. The dinosaurs would have starved or frozen to death in the conditions caused by the lack of sun.

BABY, IT'S COLD OUTSIDE!

A less dramatic explanation of extinction is that Earth's climate changed gradually and the creatures living there changed with it. Once warm and tropical, our planet's climate grew drier and cooler, which was fine for some creatures but devastating for dinosaurs, who couldn't handle the big chill.

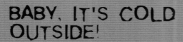

Here are some of the wackier theories about what happened to the dinosaurs:

● they ate all the plants and then starved to death

● rat-sized mammals ate all their eggs

● space aliens carried them away

What do you think?

SNAKES

SNOKES OLIVE!

Snakes are members of the reptile family, but they are much more than just legless lizards. Snakes can swim, they can tell who's about by sticking their tongues out, and they can even fly. Love them or hate them, you'll find they're not as horrific as their reputation might suggest!

▼ EGGS AND LIVE YOUNG

Most snakes lay eggs. Unlike hens' eggs, snakes' eggs feel leathery and are not hard. The majority of snakes make terrible parents, laying their eggs somewhere warm – like in rotting vegetation – and leaving their young to fend for themselves. Other snakes, such as rattlesnakes, give birth to live young. This doesn't seem to improve the relationship between mother and babies, though. After just a few days, mum leaves her young to face the world alone.

BLOWING HOT AND COLD ▶

Like other reptiles, snakes cannot generate their own body heat in the way humans do. Instead they use heat from their surroundings to get themselves moving. Sometimes they can even be spotted warming up in the early morning sun. When the temperature drops, so does their activity. Really cold weather can be lethal for snakes.

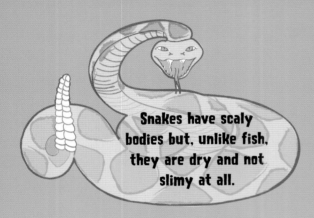

Snakes have scaly bodies but, unlike fish, they are dry and not slimy at all.

WHERE THEY ARE FOUND

As snakes are so dependent on temperature, this largely determines where they can live. Generally, snakes are found in the warmer parts of the world. Places like polar regions or the tops of mountains are just too cold. But snakes can and do live in water, including the world's oceans.

◀ BONY

Snakes get their shape from their weirdly stretched skeleton. Unlike most animals, snakes can have literally hundreds of ribs running down a backbone that reaches practically the full length of their body. What's more, in some varieties of snake, such as the python, it's possible to see a couple of little stubs of bone – the remains of legs that disappeared thousands of years ago.

23

SENSES

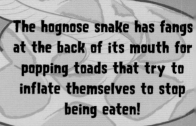

The hognose snake has fangs at the back of its mouth for popping toads that try to inflate themselves to stop being eaten!

As predators, snakes have to catch and eat other animals to live. This means they rely on their senses to spot their prey before it sees them. And snakes have some pretty spectacular ways of making sure they find lunch!

SIXTH SENSE ▼

Most animals have a maximum of five senses – sight, hearing, touch, taste and smell – but some snakes have a sixth sense: heat. Pit vipers get their name from small pits on the front of their faces that can detect very small changes in temperature. This helps the vipers to hunt warm-blooded prey, such as mice or rats, as the prey's body heat alters the temperature of the air around it.

◄ USEFUL ORGAN

Snakes don't just rely on their nostrils to smell with – they also use their tongues! If you watch a snake for any length of time, you'll notice that it is always popping its tongue in and out of its mouth. This isn't bad manners, it's because the snake is 'tasting' the air. It is bringing air into its mouth, where a cavity called the Jacobsons's organ is used to detect what is in the air particles.

▼ EAR, EAR

Snakes don't have ears, so their sense of hearing is terrible. To compensate, they are good at picking up vibrations from the ground. This lets them know if something is moving around close by.

PEEK-A-BOO! ►

Most snakes have a fairly decent sense of sight, but some types of snake can see better than others. In fact, the coachwhip snake's sense of sight is so good that it uses sight over its other senses when hunting. The trouble with snakes is that they are low to the ground and can't see far into the distance. To get around this, the snake lifts its body up into the air to peer above tall vegetation, like a periscope above the sea.

Moving about

You would think that not having any legs or arms would be a real problem when trying to get about — but not for a snake! Its long backbone and all those ribs make it very flexible. What's more, these ingenious reptiles have devised a number of different ways to get from A to B. . . .

Sea snakes have adapted to life in the water so well that they are practically helpless on land.

▼ SOMETHING FISHY

The last thing you'd expect to see underwater is a snake, but there are a few varieties that really love the water – so much so, that they spend all their lives there. Some of them, such as the Hardwicke's sea snake, have flattened tails to help push them along as they swim.

IS IT A BIRD? ▶

Why bother to climb down one tree just to climb up another one, when you can fly between them instead? The golden flying snake of southern Asia does just that, though, in truth, it's really gliding rather than flying. It launches itself from the top of a tree and flattens out its body in mid-air. This slows its fall and allows it to steer itself to a neighbouring tree.

DEADLY MUSIC

The most common way for snakes to get about is by slithering along the ground. They do this by pushing against any lumps and bumps on the floor with their belly muscles. Another method, used for sneaking up on prey, is for the snake to stretch out its body then pull the rear end back up to the front – just like a concertina, but a bit more dangerous!

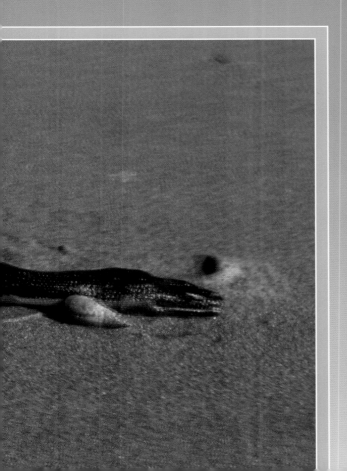

▲ SIDEWINDER

Snakes have adapted to moving in different ways depending on the type of surface they are travelling over. The sidewinder snake from the American southwest gets its name from the curious, sideways slithering way it moves. Gripping soft, sliding sand is difficult, so sidewinders, like some other desert snakes, literally throw their bodies forwards instead of slithering in the usual snakey fashion.

Bad Manners

Biting and spitting is unpleasant behaviour, but snakes have no time for social niceties. Be warned and don't tease them — they can be snappy customers!

▼ POISON

Snake poison, or 'venom', is amazing stuff. It's made up of lots of different toxins that do different jobs. Some toxins affect the heart or the muscles of the animal being bitten. Another toxin breaks down body tissue, and yet another causes internal bleeding. Poisonous snakes don't possess all these toxins at once, and not all of them cause humans too much discomfort, but it's always worth avoiding a snake bite if at all possible.

▼ FABULOUS FANGS

Snake fangs are highly developed tools – much more so than our teeth. A snake's front fangs are usually hollow, for example. This allows the snake to inject its victims with poison when it bites them. But that's not the only fang-tastic feature of snake gnashers. Pit vipers can make their fangs move. Normally the pit viper's fangs are folded away in a special pouch in the roof of its mouth, but at dinner time the snake swings them down from the pouch to bite its prey.

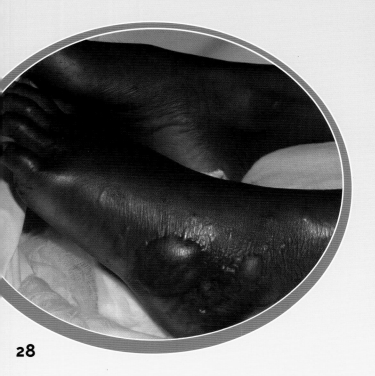

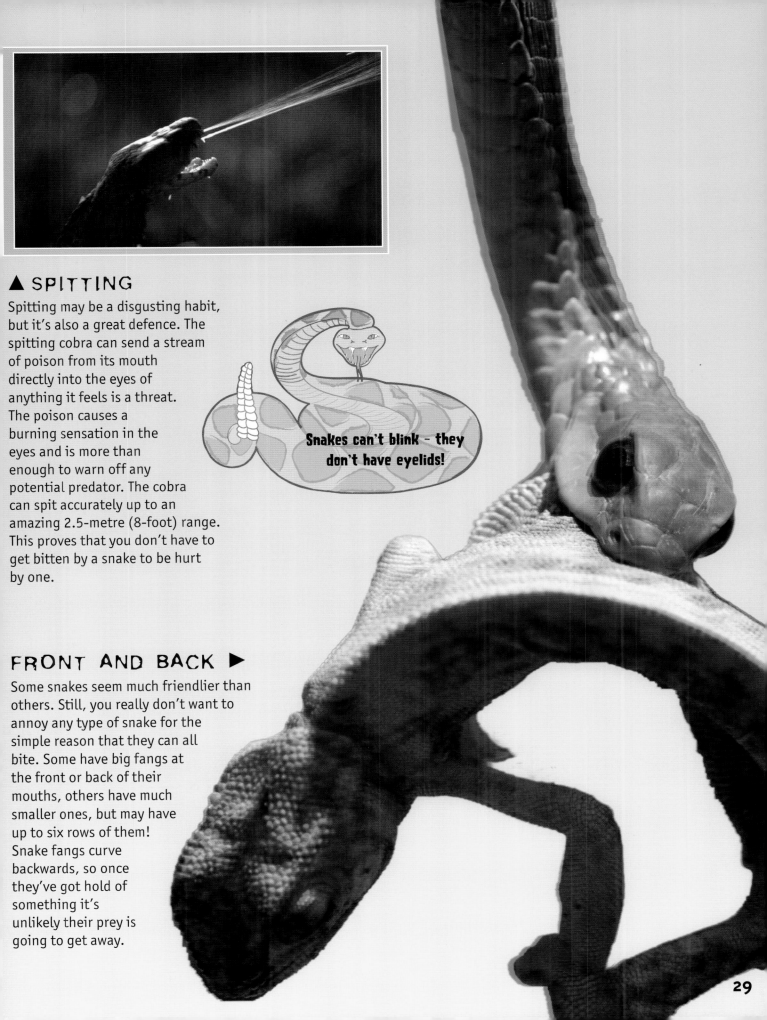

▲ SPITTING

Spitting may be a disgusting habit, but it's also a great defence. The spitting cobra can send a stream of poison from its mouth directly into the eyes of anything it feels is a threat. The poison causes a burning sensation in the eyes and is more than enough to warn off any potential predator. The cobra can spit accurately up to an amazing 2.5-metre (8-foot) range. This proves that you don't have to get bitten by a snake to be hurt by one.

Snakes can't blink - they don't have eyelids!

FRONT AND BACK ▶

Some snakes seem much friendlier than others. Still, you really don't want to annoy any type of snake for the simple reason that they can all bite. Some have big fangs at the front or back of their mouths, others have much smaller ones, but may have up to six rows of them! Snake fangs curve backwards, so once they've got hold of something it's unlikely their prey is going to get away.

Not all snakes rely on bites and poison to kill their prey. Some species of snake are known as constrictors, which means they wrap their bodies around their unfortunate victim and squeeze it to death. Constrictors don't actually crush their prey, they just squeeze it so tightly that it can't breathe and is suffocated.

TINY TERROR

Not all constrictors are giants like pythons and anacondas. Rat snakes and milk snakes also constrict their prey. Although some of these snakes grow pretty big, others are much less than one metre (3 feet) long, so they don't give larger animals much cause for concern.

THE BIGGEST OF ALL ▶

The giant of the snake world is the reticulated python. This gigantic serpent can grow over 9 metres (29.5 feet) long and is found in the Asian rainforests. Like all constrictors, pythons don't chase their prey – instead they wait in the trees to ambush their hapless victims with a lightning-quick strike, wrapping their coils around the animal before escape is possible.

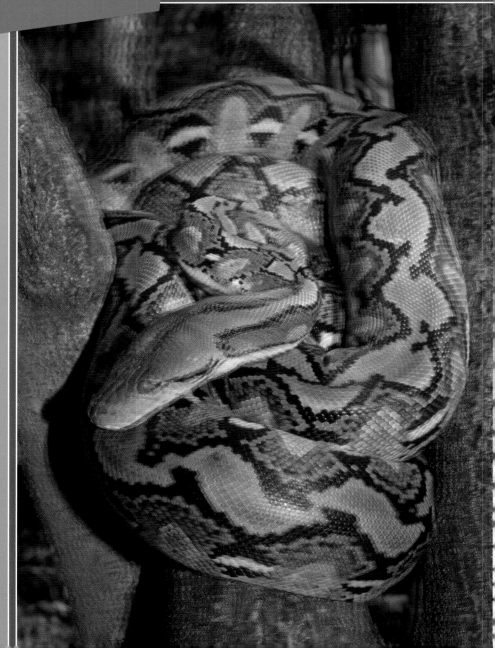

SQUEEZE

Like most snakes, constrictors are more than happy to eat their prey alive, if it's small enough.

◀ WATERY WONDER

Although not quite as long as the reticulated python, the real heavyweight of the snake world is the anaconda. In fact, anacondas are members of the boa family – the other main type of constricting snake. Anacondas are most at home in water and can be found in rivers and lakes in South America. Big enough to kill a caiman, they're the last thing you'd want to bump into when going for a swim!

▶ OPEN WIDE!

Big snakes need big meals, so most animals need to watch out for these giant predators. It is not unknown for pythons and anacondas to kill deer and wild pigs. But these snakes don't chew their food, so how does a python eat a deer? Easy – it unhinges its lower jaw and swallows the animal whole! A big meal like this can keep a snake feeling full for months.

D espite their reputation, snakes don't go looking for trouble — in fact, it's the other way round. Generally they prefer flight to fight and will go to extraordinary lengths to warn or scare away anyone or anything they think may pose some kind of threat.

HOODIES ▶

One of the best ways to scare off a predator is to make yourself look as big as possible. Cobras are particularly good at this. A cobra has a hood – a flap of skin behind its head that can be spread outwards. While extending its hood, it can raise itself up on its tail in a truly intimidating display. Cobras are highly poisonous, so the threat isn't just empty posturing.

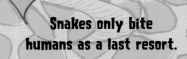

Snakes only bite humans as a last resort.

warNED!

SHAKE, RATTLE AND ROLL ▶

One of the most famous snake warning systems is the rattlesnake's rattle. The end of a rattlesnake's tail is made up of sections of loosely linked bony material. When a rattlesnake is threatened, it shakes this rattle, which produces a buzzing sound. As these snakes are poisonous, if you hear a rattle it's worth taking heed of the warning and moving yourself away from the area as quickly as possible.

◀ BEAUTIFUL, BUT DEADLY

In common with many species of animal, snakes use colour as a warning device. Generally, a snake's colourful appearance – like that of this coral snake – is a warning to predators that it is poisonous. However, this doesn't mean all colourful snakes are poisonous. Some non-poisonous snakes look like poisonous ones in order to fool predators into thinking they are deadly.

A VERY NASTY NOISE ▶

As we've seen with rattlesnakes, noise can be an effective way for a snake to let you know it's there and that it's not happy. It doesn't need a rattle to do this, of course. A well-directed hiss can be just as effective. The bullsnake is a master of the threatening hiss. When disturbed, it makes a loud hissing sound combined with a snorty grunt that sounds especially alarming!

Man bites Snake

There are hundreds of different types of snake — from tiny blind snakes to giant pythons. The biggest snakes are at the top of the food chain and have no natural predator — except people. Unfortunately, human beings are a major threat to these fabulous creatures.

Getting venom from a snake is called 'milking'.

▼ BAD MEDICINE

Snake venom can sometimes be used in modern medicine. It is possible to extract snake venom humanely, so the snake is unharmed. By pressing a snake's fangs against the edge of a jar, the poison is made to seep out. Unfortunately, the makers of some traditional medicines often use chopped-up snakes as one of their ingredients.

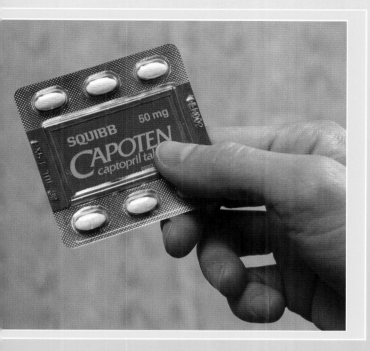

◀ KILL OR CURE

Snake venom has been used to treat illnesses for hundreds of years – generally with no beneficial effects. However, today snake venom could possibly save your life. Recently, scientists have realized there may be some value to this unorthodox treatment after all. Snake venom is now being used to create medicines that fight a whole range of illnesses, including strokes, heart disease and even cancer.

BAD PUBLICITY

Most people are scared of snakes, usually for no good reason. We know that some are poisonous enough or large enough to kill a person, and we immediately presume that snakes are out to get us. In reality, snakes are very shy, but that doesn't stop people using the bad publicity they attract as an excuse for hunting them.

▼ SAVE OUR SKIN

Unfortunately for snakes, their skin is seen as a desirable material by some clothing manufacturers. It's possible to buy snakeskin bags, belts and shoes. You can even buy jewellery made from bits of snake.

SHARKS

Shark — the very name can strike terror into people's hearts. But although sharks may seem scary, they deserve our admiration and respect. These mysterious predators of the deep have been swimming the world's oceans for over 450 million years — that's 200 million years before the dinosaurs! There are more than 375 different shark species, and still more are being discovered. Meet the undisputed masters of the deep!

▼ BONELESS FISH

Unlike most fish, whose skeletons are made of bone, sharks' skeletons are made of a tough, bendable material called cartilage – the same elastic material inside our ears and noses. Cartilage is flexible and lightweight, so sharks can swim, twist and turn quickly when chasing prey.

the deep

▲ COUSIN RAY

Although they don't look very similar, the shark's closest relatives are rays, skates and *Chimaeridae*, such as ratfish. Like their shark cousins, these fish also have skeletons of cartilage. Together they make up the class *Chondrichthyes* (Con-DRIK-thees).

The word 'shark' comes from the German word *Schurke*, meaning 'greedy parasite' or 'scoundrel'. Sailors first used the word to describe people who had swindled them.

STAYING AFLOAT

Most fish have an air sac called a swim bladder that helps keep them afloat, or buoyant, but sharks do not have one. Instead, their livers are full of oil, which is lighter than water and helps them to float. Even so, sharks are still heavier than water and need to keep swimming to stay buoyant.

▲ THAT'S ROUGH

Not only are sharks' mouths full of teeth, their skin is, too! A shark's body is covered in tiny, tooth-like scales called denticles. If you rub a shark's skin one way it feels smooth, but if you rub it in the opposite direction it is rough, like sandpaper.

Better to find

Sharks are the deadliest, most successful predators in the ocean. When they hunt, all of their senses go to work, and they are virtually unstoppable. Sharks can pick up the scent of prey in the water and track it to its source. Sharks also use a special sense of touch. Sensors called 'lateral lines' run the length of their bodies and help them detect movement and vibrations in the water. So sharks can 'feel' something without even touching it.

GIVE ME A BUZZ ▼

Sharks may not be able to detect ghosts, but they do have a sixth sense! In their snouts are tiny pores, called ampullae of Lorenzini, that can pick up the electrical pulses given off by all living things. This 'electro-sense' helps a shark pinpoint the exact location of its prey so that it can strike with amazing accuracy.

▶ SWIFT SWIMMERS

Even the shape of a shark's body helps to make it a champion predator. Almost all sharks have a curved, tapered, torpedo-shaped body, which allows them to glide smoothly – and swiftly – through the water after prey.

◀ EYE GUARD

When sinking its teeth into thrashing, struggling prey, a shark can get poked in the eye. For protection, some shark species have special eyelids, called nictitating membranes, that cover their eyes just before attack. Other sharks, like the great white, roll their eyes back into their heads.

you with!

A MAGNETIC PERSONALITY

Some sharks travel hundreds of kilometres (miles) every year to breeding and feeding grounds and never get lost. How do they find their way? Scientists aren't sure, but they think sharks may use their 'electro-sense' like a compass, to detect changes in the Earth's magnetic field.

Some sharks can smell a single drop of blood in the water half a kilometre (550 yards) away.

BETTER TO EAT

Most sharks share a similar dinner menu. They prefer smaller fish (including other sharks) and invertebrates, such as squid. Bottom-dwelling sharks, like the wobbegong or carpet shark, eat shrimps, crabs and other crustaceans living on the ocean floor. Large sharks, like the great white and the bull shark, also feed on marine mammals. Unlike most sharks, tiger sharks are famously unfussy about what they eat. They will swallow just about anything they can cram into their massive jaws!

▲ DENTAL CARE

Every time a shark eats, some of its teeth either break or fall out. Luckily, when a tooth falls out it is replaced by a tooth from the row behind. Some sharks have ten or more rows of teeth and can get through more than 20,000 teeth in a lifetime!

◄ TAKE A BITE

One of the weirdest feeders of all is the cookie-cutter shark. Its round mouth is specially designed to take cookie-sized bites out of larger animals such as whales and dolphins. The shark is about as long as a skateboard, and its 'cookie bites' are not fatal.

YOU with!

▶ FILTER FEEDERS

The largest sharks in the ocean – the whale shark, megamouth and basking shark – eat some of the ocean's smallest foods: microscopic plants and animals called plankton. Their mouths act like giant strainers to filter tiny plankton out of the water. The 10 metre-long (33-foot-long) basking shark (right) filters some 1,485,000 litres (326,650 imperial gallons) of water an hour – enough to fill a large swimming pool.

Some of the more unusual items found in a tiger shark's stomach include car registration plates, shoes, weights, tin cans and an alarm clock.

JAWS - THE FACTS

A shark's top and bottom jaws are not connected to its skull, which means it can move them out and forwards. It can therefore open its mouth really wide. The shark then snaps those powerful jaws shut round its prey, like a trap.

The 375 known shark species come in a variety of sizes and shapes, each one specially adapted to its particular lifestyle. The biggest, the whale shark, can grow to more than 15 metres (49 feet) in length, while the smallest, the pygmy shark, is less than 15 centimetres (6 inches) long and can fit in the palm of your hand. Sharks may be spotted or striped, flat-bodied or round. Some deep water sharks even glow in the dark!

The fastest shark is the shortfin mako, which can swim up to 48 kilometres (30 miles) per hour in short bursts.

▼ FUNNY FACE

Hammerhead sharks, with their strange, T-shaped heads, are easy to recognize. Their eyes, which are on either side of their broad, flat heads, give them excellent all-round vision. These sharks use their heads to pin prey, such as stingrays, to the ocean floor.

LIGHT AND SHADE

Many sharks are dark on top and pale underneath. Seen from above, they blend in with the dark waters below, and from underneath they are camouflaged against the sunlit waters above.

▲ HORNSHARK

The hornshark gets its name from the two sharp spines that stick out from its dorsal (back) fins. The spines make predators think twice before attacking. This 1-metre-long (3-foot-long) shark lives on the ocean floor off the coasts of California and Mexico.

▲ MAKE YOUR MIND UP – SPOTS OR STRIPES?

Baby zebra sharks have black and yellow stripes, but as the sharks grow the markings change into pale brown spots. The adults are therefore sometimes called leopard sharks.

◄ SPOT THE SHARK

Many bottom-dwelling sharks, like this tasselled wobbegong, are covered in spots, blotches or stripes so that they blend in with plants and rocks on the sea bed. This helps them to hide from enemies and catch unsuspecting prey.

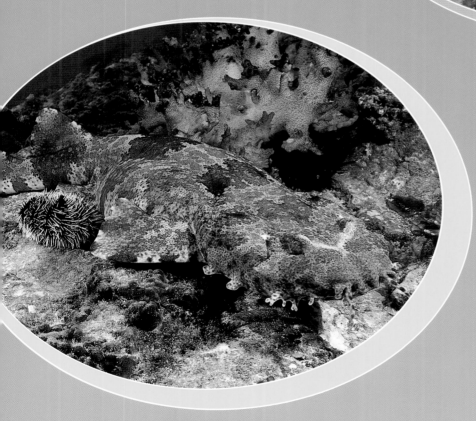

Meet the heavy

It's time to get acquainted with the most infamous shark to swim the ocean, the most feared predator in the sea — the great white. In contrast, meet the whale shark, a 'gentle giant' and the largest shark in the world. So how do these two heavyweights measure up?

▲ JAWS – THE TRUTH EXPOSED!

In 1975, the movie *Jaws* made many people afraid to go into the sea. But the great white shark in that movie could never have existed in real life. The film-makers built a mechanical shark with extra teeth and wrong-sized fins – it would sink if it were real. When real sharks were needed, small model divers were used to make the sharks seem bigger.

▲ GREAT WHITE

Scientific name: *Carcharodon carcharias*

Size: Also known as the 'white death' or the 'white pointer', the great white is the largest flesh-eating shark. It is about 6 metres (20 feet) long and weighs over 2 tonnes (tons).

Colouring: It has a very distinctive two-tone colouring. Its upper body is blue to grey, while its underbelly is much lighter, sometimes even white.

Range: The great white shark lives in cool waters in subtropical and temperate seas.

Diet: With its 5-cm-long (2-inch-long) serrated teeth, the great white eats fish and sea mammals like seals and sea lions.

WEIGHTS

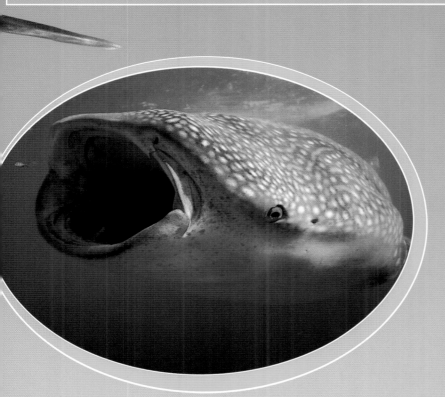

▲ BIG MOUTH, TINY TEETH
The whale shark's mouth is lined with thousands of tiny teeth, each one about the size of a grain of rice.

▲ WHALE SHARK
Scientific name: *Rhincodon typus*

Size: It is named after its size. Measuring over 14 metres (46 feet) in length and weighing more than 13 tonnes (13 tons), the whale shark is the largest shark, and the largest fish, in the world.

Colouring: On top it is blue-grey, but underneath it is white. Its skin is camouflaged with distinctive white spots and bars to help it blend in with the dappled water.

Range: The whale shark lives in warm waters on either side of the Equator, both in the open ocean and near the shore.

Diet: Plankton. The shark flushes huge mouthfuls of water over its gill rakers (walls of spongy mesh inside its throat). The gill rakers act as a sieve, trapping the plankton for the shark to swallow.

S.O.S.—save

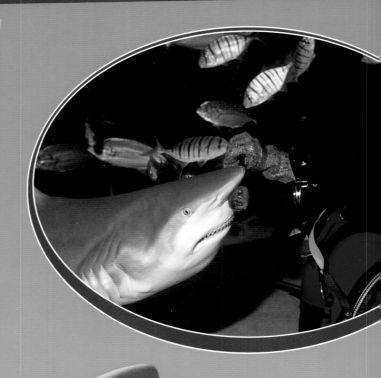

So many sharks are killed each year that several kinds, including the great white, blue and basking shark, are in big trouble. They are classified as threatened species, meaning their numbers are dwindling so rapidly that conservationists warn they could soon be in danger of dying out altogether. If shark species went extinct, all ocean life would suffer. As top-of-the-food-chain predators, sharks keep many fish populations in check; as scavengers, sharks help keep the oceans clean.

▲ HEALTH SHARKS

Sharks don't lose many days to sickness because they don't often get diseases. Finding out how sharks stay so healthy could help humans discover how to avoid serious diseases, such as cancer.

◀ SPIRITS OF THE DEEP

Sharks are important symbols for indigenous peoples around the world. In Hawaii, people believed that the shark god Kamohoali would help lost fishermen by leading their canoes through fog and mist. Some Pacific islanders believe that sharks are the spirits of their dead ancestors.

Our sharks

We must help change the shark's reputation as a ruthless man-eater so that these amazing creatures are respected and preserved.

▼ WHAT IS BEING DONE?

Many marine biologists and conservation groups are working hard to make sure we don't hunt our sharks to extinction. Biologists study sharks in their natural environment to learn more about their behaviour and life history. The more we know about sharks, the more we can do to help save them. Conservation groups spread the word about sharks in danger and put pressure on governments to pass laws protecting them. They also set up underwater nature reserves where sharks can live without danger of being fished by humans.

SAFELY BEHIND GLASS

Aquariums play a part in helping sharks. By offering visitors a close-up view of live sharks, they help us understand how beautiful and unique they are and how important it is to protect them.

REPTILES

What do you think of when you hear the word 'reptile'? Many people think of cold, slimy snakes. True, snakes are reptiles, but they aren't cold or slimy, and they are just one member of a huge family of weird and wonderful reptilian creatures. There are more than seven thousand types of reptile and they come in all shapes and sizes, from giant lizards and huge tortoises to the tiniest of geckos.

MEET THE ANCESTORS ▶

Even the biggest of today's lizards don't match up to their huge predecessors, the dinosaurs. That's right – those mighty monsters from the past were reptiles, too. So the next time a snake gives you the shivers or a turtle gives you a fright, be thankful it isn't a *T. rex* instead! In fact, reptiles were around long before the dinosaurs appeared. The oldest fossil reptile found to date is more than 340 million years old.

PTILE?

BIG AND SMALL ▼

Although today's reptiles aren't as big as dinos, they still come in a wide range of sizes. Anacondas, giant South American snakes, can grow to between 8–11 metres (26–36 feet) long – that's about the length of two-and-a-half family cars. At the other end of the scale, the smallest reptiles are geckos. Some geckos grow no longer than around 2.5 centimetres (1 inch).

People who study reptiles are called **herpetologists.**

SUN LOVERS ▶

Reptiles can be found virtually anywhere, from high-rise buildings in Los Angeles, or deserts in Africa, to the depths of the Indian Ocean. But you won't find reptiles in most Arctic areas or in Antarctica. This is because they don't like the cold. So don't worry about bumping into one on a ski slope!

Body bits

So, what makes a reptile what it is? Although they may look very different from one another, all reptiles have some things in common — even if it doesn't look like it at first.

▼ NOT GOOD IN THE MORNING

Reptiles are often described as cold-blooded, which means they can't generate their own body heat. Instead, they have to rely on the sun to warm them up. Reptiles are very sluggish when they haven't warmed up enough, and this makes it easy for predators to catch them. The hotter the climate, the quicker a reptile can warm up, which is why they don't live in cold places.

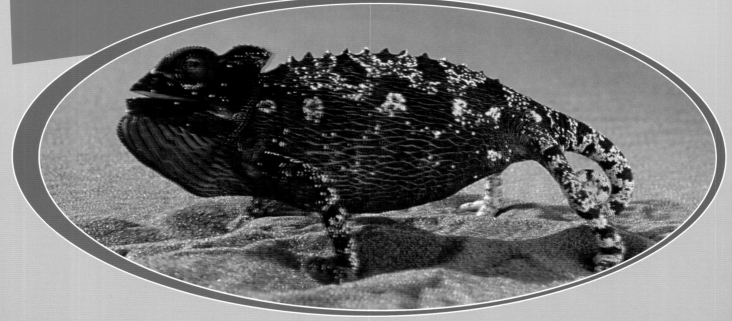

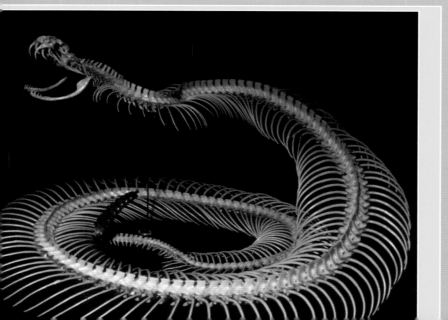

◄ BITS AND PIECES

All reptiles have a skeleton with a backbone. They all also lay eggs, which have a waterproof shell. Remarkably, all reptiles have four legs, or have ancestors who had four legs — even snakes! Of course snakes lost their legs a long time ago, but their ancestors had them and you can see boney traces of legs on the skeletons of some snakes.

SCALES ▼

All reptiles have scales made from keratin – the same stuff as human fingernails. Their skin is very dry. It provides a barrier to moisture and stops reptiles losing water from their bodies. In some reptiles, such as crocodiles, the scales on the skin surface fuse together to form plates. This makes the skin very tough.

Reptiles can virtually shut down their bodies if they get too cold.

GOING UP ▶

Some reptiles have special feet which makes them great climbers. Clawed feet are an obvious help. Some lizards, such as geckos, have millions of little hairs, called 'setae', on the bottom of their feet. These tiny hairs allow geckos to climb walls with the greatest of ease.

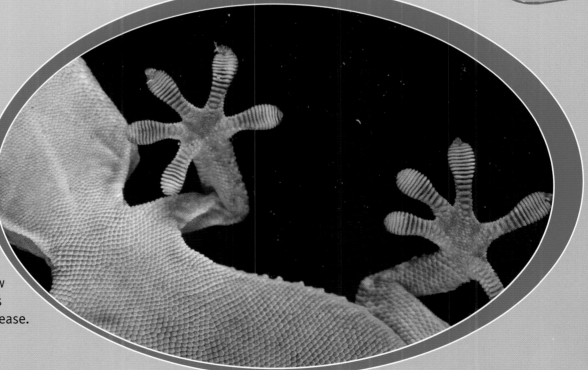

Here be dra

W hen people first found fossils, they imagined they must be the bones of monsters or dragons. Then, when explorers and traders went to far off countries and saw some of the biggest and most fearsome-looking reptiles, they came home with even taller tales of enormous beasts. They may not be gigantic, but these modern-day monsters are still impressive creatures.

It was once believed that a stare from a basilisk lizard was enough to kill you!

▼ WORTH MONITORING

The heavyweights of the lizard world are the monitors, and king among them is the Komodo dragon. Found only on Komodo and other neighbouring islands, these fearsome creatures grow to over 3 metres (10 feet) and weigh more than two people. They are big enough to kill and eat deer and have even been known to eat children!

ᴑONS

▼ PROUD PARENTS

Crocodiles might be the last thing you'd want to see when you go swimming, but they are great parents. One of the few members of the reptile family to take care of their young, crocodiles make nests for their eggs and, when their babies hatch, take care of them. Some species even carry their babies from the nest to the water in their mouth – and aren't tempted to eat a single one!

▲ SNEAKY SNAPPER

There are over 20 species of crocodilian, including crocodiles, alligators and caimans. The biggest are saltwater crocodiles, who can grow to over 6 metres (20 feet) in length and weigh more than a car. Crocodilians are good at hiding in the water and ambushing their prey. They sneak up on their victims while they are drinking, then lunge out of the water to grab them. Some species can even jump out of the water and straight up in the air.

NOT A PRETTY SIGHT ▶

The marine iguana is so odd-looking that even the renowned naturalist, Charles Darwin, described it as 'disgusting'. However, he was probably impressed by its swimming skills, as this strange lizard can stay underwater for up to an hour.

SNAKES RULE

S nakes come right at the top of the list of things that people are scared of. But their fearsome reputation is unfair, as most people with a snake phobia have never seen one. In reality, snakes aren't at all like you'd imagine. They're very shy creatures and would much rather scurry away from you than attack you. Many snakes are harmless, and even the most poisonous ones will only bite if provoked or surprised.

▼ FANG-TASTIC

Poisonous snakes don't have the biggest fangs you're likely to see in the animal kingdom, but they're very good at using them. Like hypodermic needles, snakes' fangs are perfect for injecting poison into their prey.

If you see a snake with large fangs like this, you can be sure that it's a poisonous one.

HOODED KING ▶

The most famous venomous snake is the cobra, with its distinctive hood of skin behind its head. The largest of the cobra family is the king cobra, which is so venomous that it can kill an elephant with a single bite.

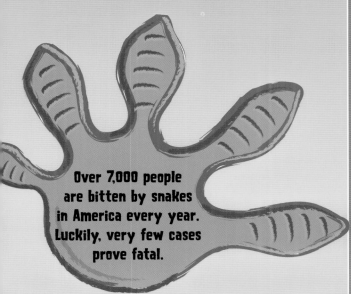

▼ GULP!

Snakes have very flexible jaws. When it comes to meal times, snakes open their mouths as wide as possible and swallow their prey whole – always head first, as it's easier to swallow that way.

▲ BIG SQUEEZE

The biggest snakes of all – boas and pythons – are not venomous. They don't need to be – in place of poison, they use their coils to squeeze their victims to death.

Over 7,000 people are bitten by snakes in America every year. Luckily, very few cases prove fatal.

Hard shell

Y ou might know them as slow-moving lettuce chompers, and certainly tortoises and turtles don't seem to be in much of a hurry. Nevertheless, the chelonian family includes a lot of remarkable animals. Some species journey thousands of kilometres (miles) across oceans, others can live longer than almost any other animal on Earth. Meet a truly terrific family of tortoises, turtles and terrapins!

▲ HARD CASE

All members of the chelonian family have a shell. The shell is part of the turtle's skeleton and is generally very hard and protective. Some chelonians can even bring their legs, head and tail into the shell for extra protection. But not all chelonian shells are hard. The leatherback turtle, for example, has a soft shell. This is because the turtle swims to great depths in the sea, where the water pressure would crack a hard shell.

WHAT'S WHAT? ▶

All chelonians are turtles, but people tend to call different ones by different names. As a rule, a tortoise lives on land and a turtle lives in the water. In the UK, a turtle that lives in fresh water is called a terrapin.

FLIPPING BRILLIANT ▼

There are over 250 species of turtles and tortoises, and many of them spend their time in water. But only seven species of turtle live all the time in the ocean. These sea turtles, like this loggerhead turtle, have large flippers instead of legs to help them swim, and only visit dry land to lay their eggs.

▲ UNDER THREAT

Like many reptiles, turtles are under threat. Loss of habitat, hunting, poaching and pollution are slowly killing off some species of these ancient, stately creatures. In some countries, it is now illegal to have a tortoise as a pet unless it has been born in the same country.

GENTLE GIANTS ▶

Some of the most famous tortoises of all are those found on the Galapagos Islands in the Pacific Ocean. These giants can measure over 1 metre (3 feet) from head to tail and weigh more than 200 kilograms (440 pounds). Even more remarkably, these gentle giants can live for between 150 and 200 years.

Frills and sp

With so many different types of reptile, it should come as no surprise that some of them look a little odd. And, at times, they behave as strangely as they look!

▼ WALKING ON WATER

If the basilisk lizard is in a hurry and finds there is water in its path, it won't swim across or look for another route. Instead, it picks up speed and runs across the top of the water on its hind legs. This miraculous behaviour has earned it the name of the Jesus lizard.

▲ BUG-EYED MARVEL

The chameleon is a remarkable beast. Not only does it have popping-out eyes, which can move in opposite directions to each other, and a long tongue, which can shoot out to catch flies, it can also change colour. It is often thought that chameleons change colour to blend in with their background. But some scientists believe that chameleons do it to show anger or fear.

Some lizards' tails snap off if they're captured, leaving them free to escape.

ILLS

▶ TREE HOPPER

You will find reptiles underground, up in trees, on the water, in the water and even in the air. Some tree-dwelling lizards have taken to springing into the air to get to neighbouring trees. Although they are called flying dragons, these reptiles in fact use special flaps of skin to help them sail, like a hang-glider, from tree to tree.

PUTTING ON A SHOW ▶

If reptiles feel threatened, the first thing they do is try to get away. If reptiles are cornered, however, they have different ways of reacting. Some reptiles play dead; and rattlesnakes shake the tip of their tails to make a rattling noise as a warning. One of the most startling displays is made by the frilled lizard of Australia. This lizard spreads out a frill around its head and hisses at the animal chasing it. The frill makes the lizard look much bigger than it is and, hopefully, puts off the attacker.

KILLER CATS

What is a big

The history of the cat stretches back over 30 million years, and today there are over 30 different species. At the top of this feline pile are the big cats. Although this is a rather general group, when people talk about big cats they often mean tigers, lions, leopards, cheetahs, cougars and jaguars.

▲ WHAT BIG TEETH YOU HAVE

One of the most famous cats was the sabre-tooth, which died out about 10,000 years ago. This fearsome predator had a massive pair of pointy teeth, which it used to stab its prey.

▲ SAME DIFFERENCE

From the humble tabby to the majestic lion, all cats are basically the same. They all have excellent senses of smell and sight, and they like to keep clean. All cats are carnivores, too, which means they are meat-eaters – and the bigger the cat, the bigger the meal it needs.

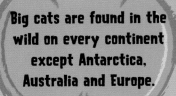

Big cats are found in the wild on every continent except Antarctica, Australia and Europe.

cat?

▲ ENDANGERED SPECIES

Despite being top predators, many species of big cat are under threat of extinction. Some cats are hunted for their skins, which are used to make clothes or rugs, others are killed for their bones and teeth, which are used in some traditional medicines. Even though these cats are protected, they are still hunted by poachers.

▲ NOW YOU SEE THEM

Whether spotty or stripy, or a plain dusty brown colour, each cat's coat serves the same purpose – it helps the animal to hide. All big cats have to catch their food, so the longer they can stay hidden from their prey, the more chance they have of sneaking up and catching it.

SAVING THE CATS ▶

Many organizations are trying to protect big cats. One way to do this is to educate people so that they know how important big cats are to the local economy. A dead cat can bring big money for poachers, but a live cat brings in more from rich tourists who want to see it in the wild. Also, farmers don't mind losing cattle so much if they are paid for each animal that gets eaten by a cat.

Tigers

With its orangey-red stripey body, the tiger is the most recognizable of all the big cats. It is also the biggest, with the Siberian, or Amur tiger being the biggest species of all. These huge cats can grow up to 4 metres (13 feet) in length and weigh as much as four people. Tigers can be found in India, Siberia, and Southeast Asia. There are five types of tiger alive today, but there used to be more species spread across a much bigger area.

▲ GOOD MOTHER

Like most big cats, tigers are solitary creatures, except when a mother tiger is raising her young. Tiger cubs stay with their mother for around two years before leaving to find their own territories. During those years, the mother teaches her cubs how to survive in the wild. One of the most important lessons is how to stalk and hunt prey – if you don't eat, you don't survive.

◄ MAN HUNTER

Tigers are one of the few big cats who will occasionally hunt people as their prey. This is particularly true in the Sunderban region of Bengal, India. This large area is made up of mangrove trees growing where three rivers meet the sea. People don't actually live there, but they visit to collect wood and to hunt. Tigers kill people in this region every year. Knowing that tigers like to sneak up on their prey, the wily locals started wearing masks on the backs of their heads so a tiger creeping up from behind would think it had been seen.

▲ FANCY A DIP?

Like pet cats, some big cats hate the water. Not the tiger though, who likes nothing better than a relaxing swim in a cool river or pond.

No two tigers have the same stripey pattern on their coats. Each tiger's coat is unique – a bit like your fingerprints.

LIONS

The lion is often called the king of the beasts, and it's easy to see why. Although it's true that lions are not the biggest cats in the world, they are certainly kings of all they survey in their own territories. Lions used to be found in Africa, Asia and even Europe, but are now restricted to India and Africa.

▲ SOCIABLE CATS

Lions are social animals, which makes them something of a rarity in the cat world. They are the only cats to live in family groups, called prides. The head of the pride is the dominant male lion.

▲ TEAM WORK

Lions are not the fastest of the big cats. You would think this might be a problem when chasing down speedy gazelles or swift zebras. However, lions get round this by hunting as a team. Generally, the lionesses do all the hunting, but when it comes to eating, the males eat first. That doesn't really seem fair, does it?

◄ SLIM PICKINGS

Even though lions are sociable, it's still a tough life for the cubs. They are always last to feed after a kill and some cubs have been known to starve to death if there's not enough meat to go round. Worse still, if a new lion becomes the pride's dominant male he is likely to kill the cubs of the old male.

Strangely, lion cubs are born with spots. As the cubs get older, the spots disappear.

◄ MANE ATTRACTION

Male lions are the only members of the cat family to have a mane. Nobody is exactly sure what it's for, but many scientists presume it's for making the lion look good and attracting lionesses. Interestingly, a recent study found that the darker the lion's mane, the more attractive the lion was to females.

LEOpards

The leopard is one adaptable cat — it can live in all sorts of different environments and will hunt many types of animal, from lizards to baby giraffes. It is also the most widespread of the big cats and comes in a whole range of different sizes, depending on where it lives. Leopards are found in Africa, India, Siberia, China and Indonesia. They can live in forests, grasslands, and even mountainous areas, depending on the country.

BLACK PANTHER ▶

Some leopards are born almost completely black in colour and are sometimes known as panthers. No one knows why this is, but there seem to be more panthers born in areas with thick jungle. Perhaps a dark coat is even harder to see here. If you look closely at the coat you will see that it has dark spots and rings, called rosettes.

▼ DISAPPEARING TRICK

A leopard's coat is covered in rosettes. This odd patterning is excellent for helping it hide in trees or long grass. In fact the leopard is one of the stealthiest hunters on the planet and an expert at creeping right up on its prey without the unfortunate animal realizing.

▲ DIFFERENT VARIETIES

There are more than 20 species or subspecies of leopard, and they come in all sorts of shapes and sizes. In fact, some scientists believe that two sorts of leopard, the clouded leopard of the Indonesian islands and the snow leopard of Siberia, are so different from normal leopards that they should be classed as a separate species.

Some leopards' rosettes are a roundish shape and others are square, depending on where the leopard is from.

► FOLLOW ME

Being so good at hiding does have its downside – it makes it very difficult for your cubs to find you or follow you in the grass. Leopards overcome this problem by having bright white patches behind their ears, which the cubs find easy to spot.

Cheetahs

The cheetah is the great specialist of the cat world and has become a lightning-fast hunting machine. Once found throughout Africa, the Middle East and India, now these sleek, speedy animals are an endangered species. It used to be thought that cheetahs could only hunt on the open plains of the African savannah, but cheetahs are also found in mountainous areas. There are cheetahs in many parts of Africa, and there may even be a small population of cheetahs in Iran.

Cheetahs have two large black lines running down their faces from their eyes, which make them look as though they are crying.

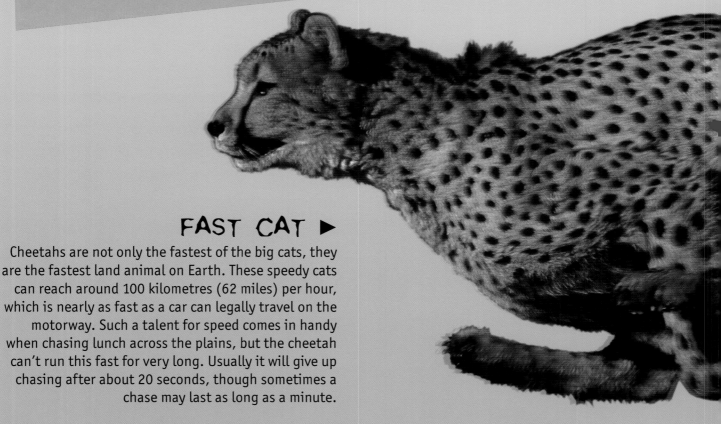

FAST CAT ▶

Cheetahs are not only the fastest of the big cats, they are the fastest land animal on Earth. These speedy cats can reach around 100 kilometres (62 miles) per hour, which is nearly as fast as a car can legally travel on the motorway. Such a talent for speed comes in handy when chasing lunch across the plains, but the cheetah can't run this fast for very long. Usually it will give up chasing after about 20 seconds, though sometimes a chase may last as long as a minute.

▲ HEY, THAT'S MINE!

Extreme speed has its downside. The cheetah is quite a lightweight cat, which is great for travelling fast and catching prey, but bad for fighting. Often a cheetah will catch its prey, only to have it stolen by a bigger, meaner predator such as a lion, hyena or even a baboon. No wonder cheetahs always seem to be crying!

▲ ROYAL CONNECTIONS

Cheetahs are one of the easiest cats to tame and were once the fashionable pets of ancient royalty. It is believed that cheetahs have been caught as pets for over 5,000 years. Cheetahs were used as hunting cats by monarchs and emperors from Sumeria to Europe, who used the cats' awesome speed to catch other animals.

CHEEP! CHEEP!

Cheetahs don't roar, like some of the big cats. Instead they make an odd little noise which sounds like chirping. When they are annoyed, they hiss, and when they are happy, cheetahs make a loud purring noise – just like big tabby cats.

Cougars

The sleek and athletic cougar is the most widespread of American big cats. In some parts of America it is still legal to hunt these magnificent animals, though many people are trying to stop this practice. Cougars are found from southern Canada to Patagonia in South America. However, their distribution is patchy, and many populations have become isolated by new housing developments that have blocked the links between the areas they inhabit.

▲ FACE TO FACE

Occasionally, people and cougars come face to face. If this happens to you, the trick is to make yourself look as big as possible and stare the cougar straight in the eye. If you're wearing a jacket, spread it out like a cape behind you. Never bend down, as this makes you look more like cougar food. Never take your eyes off the cat and don't turn your back on it.

◄ OH, SO SECRET!

Even though cougars live across a huge area of North and South America, very few people have seen them in the wild. There are a couple of reasons for this. Firstly, cougars hunt at dawn, dusk and night, so there are fewer people around at those times to see them. Secondly, cougars are very shy animals and will usually go out of their way to avoid people.

BURIED TREASURE ▶

Once a cougar has made a kill, it wants to keep hold of it. It cleverly buries its prize under a pile of leaves and dirt. With its food safely hidden, the cougar returns every night until it's all been eaten.

Cougars are called a variety of names, including puma, mountain lion and Florida panther.

A PAIN IN THE NECK ▶

Cougars aren't fussy about their food and will eat almost anything, from deer to insects. They sneak up on their prey in the same way that other big cats do. When the cougar gets close, it pounces on its victim with one mighty leap. However, unlike other big cats, a cougar doesn't strangle its prey but breaks its neck with a bite from its powerful jaws.

Jaguars

The greatest South American predator is the jaguar. Like the leopard, the jaguar is a stealthy night hunter, using its excellent night vision to track prey. The jaguar lives on its own and is an expert at hiding in the trees or bushes. Like leopards, some jaguars have black fur. Jaguars are most common in forested areas of South and Central America, but can also be found in southwestern parts of North America.

▼ HEADACHE

Unlike most big cats, the jaguar does not kill its prey by biting it round the neck and suffocating it. Instead, the jaguar uses its powerful jaws and sharp teeth to bite its prey in the head.

◄ GONE FISHING

Jaguars eat a wide range of animals, from deer to crocodilians. Jaguars have also developed an ingenious method of fishing. The cat waits by the water and splashes the surface every so often with its tail. For some reason, this attracts fish, which the jaguar promptly scoops out of the water with its paws.

SPOT THE DIFFERENCE ►

Jaguars are often confused with leopards, but they live on different continents and are a heavier and stockier cat. There is also a subtle difference to their spotty coats. Both jaguars and leopards have a spotty, rosette pattern, but it's the inside of the rosettes that give the game away – jaguars have a few smaller spots inside the rosettes, leopards don't.

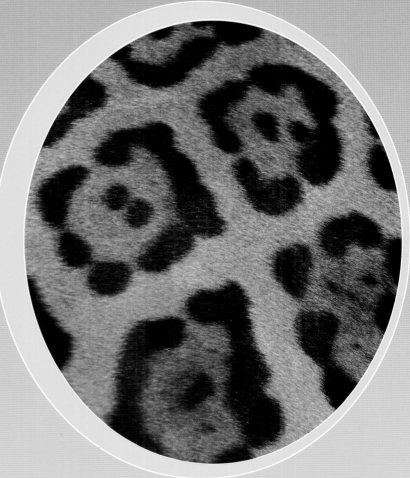

Tribespeople often call the jaguar 'the beast that kills its prey with one bound'.

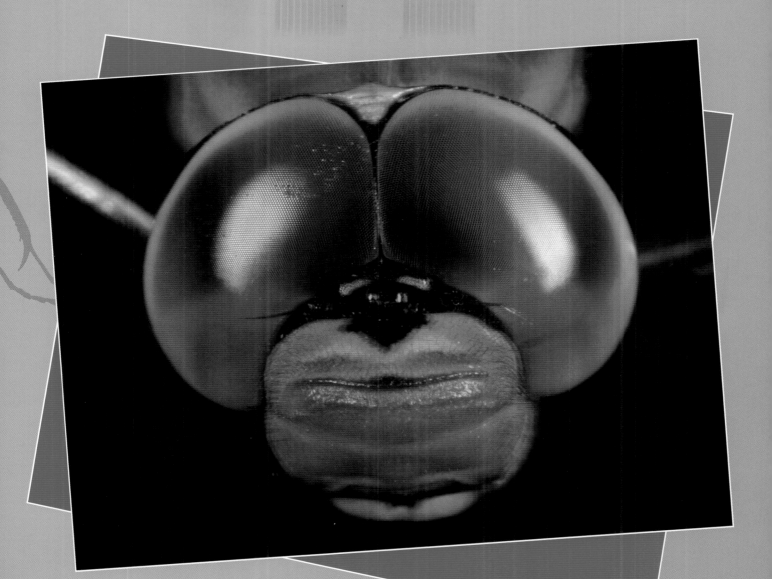

BUGS

What is a bug?

Bugs, creepy crawlies, minibeasts — call them what you will — many people don't seem to have a high opinion of these mini-marvels of the animal world. This is really unfair, for a lot of reasons. Bugs are so useful that life on our planet depends on them. So, like them or loathe them, you'll definitely be amazed by these brilliant beasties.

There are more different species of insect in the world than any other type of animal.

▼ SURVIVORS

Bugs are the great survivors of the animal kingdom. They can withstand any temperature and some, such as cockroaches, will eat practically anything. Cockroaches also have a tough body, which makes them difficult to kill, and they breed very quickly. This combination makes them the animal most likely to be around long after most other ones have disappeared.

▼ BIG GROUP

Often when people talk about bugs, they mean a group of animals called arthropods. This group includes insects, which have three body parts and six legs — beetles, ants and wasps are all insects. The arthropod group also includes arachnids, such as spiders, and crustaceans like wood lice.

▲ SLOW MOVERS

The loose term 'bug' can also include another group
of creatures called gastropods. You and I would call
them slugs and snails, and most people would
definitely call them creepy crawlies.

▲ROUND THE WORLD

Bugs are superbly adaptable, so no matter where you
are in the world you are sure to find bugs there, too.
You'll see bugs in forests, cities, in the air and under
water. Bugs can cope with heat, so you'll find them
in the desert. They're good in the cold, too, so you
can even find some of them at the poles.

BIG NUMBERS

How many bugs are there in the world? Well, it's
difficult to tell as there are new species
being discovered all the time. Estimates
vary between six and nine million
different species, but some
scientists put the figure
much higher than this,
possibly as high
as 30 million
different species.

SENSES

Just like us, bugs can hear, see, taste, smell and feel things. But as bugs look very different from us, they also experience all these things in a different way, too.

We humans find two eyes more than enough to get about with, but not spiders. These web-spinning wonders don't just have eight legs, they also have eight eyes!

▼ EYE EYE!

Many bugs have what are called 'compound' eyes. Their eyes are made up of lots of little hexagonal shapes. Each hexagon sees a different bit of what is in front of the bug, and the bug's brain puts together all the little viewpoints like a jigsaw so it can see the big picture. The bigger a bug's eyes, the better it can see, so a dragonfly's gigantic eyes give it great sight.

▼ TASTY

It will come as no surprise that bugs use different bits of their bodies to taste with. Some bugs use their mouths like we do. Other bugs, such as some flies and butterflies, use their feet. Imagine standing in your food before eating it – that's the trouble with bugs, no table manners!

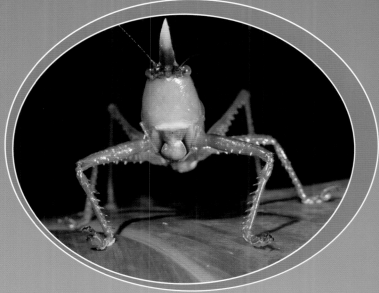

I CAN HEAR YOU ▲

Bugs don't have ears as we know them. Instead they hear with different parts of their bodies. Many insects have fine hairs on their bodies that pick up the tiny vibrations made by sound. This does not necessarily mean they can hear, though. Crickets, however, can definitely hear – they pick up sounds through small holes in their forelegs.

▼ TOUCHY FEELY

Some scientists believe that bugs with poor eyesight, such as bees, rely on the stalks on their heads, called antennae, to feel objects – and one another. Some bugs use the hairs on their bodies to feel movement.

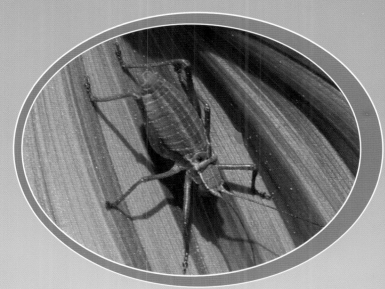

WHAT A RACKET! ▲

Very few bugs can actually make noise, but some do. Grasshoppers make their familiar sound by rubbing their back legs against their forewings. Crickets and *katydids* (relatives of crickets) rub their forewings together. The Madagascan hissing cockroach makes a loud hiss when it expels air through tiny holes in its body. And the cicada flexes its body in and out to produce its famous click.

Getting about

Bugs have developed different ways of getting around because they live in different environments. For example, there's no point having wings if you spend all your life underground. So whether it's the expert flying of the dragonfly, the slow slide of the slug or the frantic scurrying of ants, each method of getting about suits the way that particular bug lives.

SLIP-SLIDING AWAY ▶

If you only had one foot to get about on, you'd think hopping would be your only way of moving. Not for snails and slugs, though – these amazing creatures have one long foot, which they squeeze in and out to move. The slimy trail they leave is mucus, a substance that helps them to slide over rough or sharp ground without getting injured.

How can you tell millipedes and centipedes apart? Millipedes have four legs for every body segment, centipedes only have two.

► HAVE WINGS, WILL TRAVEL

The best way of covering long distances is to take to the air. This could be why many bugs have wings. And some bugs *really* get about. A desert locust can travel thousands of kilometres (miles) in its lifetime. However, the top travellers of the bug world must be monarch butterflies – some fly from Mexico to Canada and back every year.

◄ JUMP AROUND

Why bother to walk, though, when it's much quicker to jump? Many insects, such as froghoppers, can jump, as it's a useful way of avoiding trouble or hunting for food. The king of the jumping world is the flea. Fleas can jump over 100 times their own height – that would be like us jumping over the Washington Monument or the London Eye!

LOTS OF LEGS ►

Most bugs have six legs, others have eight, which might seem enough for anybody. Not centipedes and millipedes, though, which can usually have between 100 and 400 legs. It is believed that some species of millipede have up to 750 legs. Just imagine having an itchy foot – you'd never be able to work out which one it was!

Hiding or scar

Like all other animals, bugs spend much of their time looking for something to eat, and avoiding being eaten at the same time. It really is a matter of life and death — and some bugs go to surprising lengths to make sure they're still around at the end of the day.

Not all bugs want to hide, some are very bright colours – this usually tells other animals that the bug doesn't taste nice. You wouldn't want to get eaten by mistake, would you?

▼ NASTY SURPRISE

No web-building for the crab spider! This sneaky predator lies in wait inside flowers to ambush its prey. It doesn't just hide, though; it can also change its colour to match the flower it's hiding in. Not all bugs have good eyesight, so the spider doesn't often go hungry.

NOT A PRAYER! ▲

The easiest way to hunt is to get your prey to come to you. As many bugs spend their lives on twigs and stalks, it makes sense for them to look like the host plant so that they can catch their food easily. The praying mantis is an expert at this, blending in perfectly with its surroundings, staying still and waiting to catch its prey.

iNg

► WHERE'S IT GONE?

Butterflies, moths and caterpillars are hiding experts. The aptly named dead leaf butterfly is a good example. When it folds its brightly coloured wings together, the dull undersides of the wings are the colour of a dead leaf. The wings are even leaf-shaped, too, to help the transformation.

▲ HERE I AM!

A different approach to avoiding predators is to look like a bigger, fiercer animal. The hawk moth caterpillar, for example, has markings at its back end which look a bit like a snake. When it feels threatened, it waves this end around to make the snake impression even more convincing.

DROPPING OUT ►

The trouble with being a bug is that you're generally snack-sized as far as many other animals are concerned. The best way not to get eaten is to look like something you wouldn't want to eat. And surely the giant swallowtail butterfly caterpillar wins the unappetizing meal competition – it looks exactly like a bird dropping!

Ganging Up

Many bugs live in huge extended families, called colonies. The advantages of living in a group are obvious. There are more of you to look for food, to help protect the home from attack, and to look after the young bugs and eggs.

▼ HIGH-RISE HOME

A big family needs a big house, of course, and few bug houses come much bigger than a termites' mound. The mounds can be over 4 metres (13 feet) high, and are built over the termites' nest, which is buried underground. The mound is made of dried mud, and protects the nest from overheating, or getting too cold, or from too much rain getting in.

ORDERED SOCIETY ▲

Bugs that live in big groups tend to be very well organized, with different types of bug doing different jobs. Bees are a good example of this. At the top of the pile is the queen, who lays all the eggs. Next are the drones, who mate with the queen. At the bottom of the pile are the worker bees, who find all the nectar to make honey. Worker bees are also expected to feed the queen and the young bees, and protect the hive from attack. It's no fun being at the bottom of the pile!

◄ MESSING AROUND ON THE WATER

You would think the last place you would expect to find an ant is on a river. However, if fire ants get flooded out of their home, they think nothing of grouping together in a big cluster and floating down the river. They'll drift about until they land somewhere drier where they can make a new home.

Millions of termites can live in a single mound at the same time. That's one sociable species!

▼ DEADLY SWARM

Sometimes, bugs that normally live alone gather together in huge groups with devastating effect. A single locust – a large, flying plant-eater – is not much of a problem. However, if a few locusts get together they can start giving off signals that might attract many more, until hundreds of thousands appear. When this huge swarm gets hungry, it can strip fields bare for miles around.

HELPING OUT

Bugs may be on the small side, but don't underestimate how useful they are. If there were no bugs in the world, nothing else would survive. For a start, they pollinate flowers; but they are also Mother Nature's rubbish disposal brigade. Dead plants, dead animals and even animal droppings are got rid of by these hard-working helpers.

Some American beekeepers hire out their hives to fruit farmers, who use the bees to pollinate their fruit trees.

▼ DIRTY JOB

One of the most important insects on the planet has one of the most unpleasant jobs to do. The dung beetle takes other animals' poo and uses it to lay its eggs in, or even eats it. This might sound disgusting, but if dung beetles didn't do it we'd all be buried under a huge mound of the stinky stuff. It's a dirty job, but someone's got to do it!

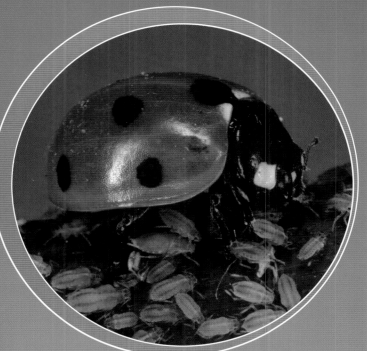

▼ BAD BUGS

So why do bugs have such a bad reputation? Partly, it's down to fear – loads of people get a fright from a spider in the bath-tub, for example. Also, it's because people don't like bugs doing what they do. Fleas, for example, need to feed on blood. But when that blood comes from humans or their pets, then the flea becomes public enemy number one. Finally, some bugs, such as mosquitoes, can pass on harmful illnesses or diseases.

▲ GARDENER'S FRIEND

As we have already seen, some bugs eat other bugs. This is good news for gardeners, as it means they can help to protect their plants by encouraging friendly bugs to visit. One of the best bugs gardeners can find on their plants is the ladybird, because adult ladybirds can eat up to fifty plant-chomping aphids a day.

◄ NEW NUTRIENTS

Soil needs feeding just like you or me. Soil gets its rich nutrients from rotting vegetation. Insects such as millipedes and ground beetles are great at eating dead plants and leaves. When these insects have a poo, it's full of dead plant nutrients which go into the soil and are used by plants for their essential growth.

Massive to

As there are so many bugs, it'll be no surprise to hear that they come in all sorts of shapes and sizes. Bugs can be so small you need a microscope to see them. Or they can be more than big enough to give you a nasty fright if you aren't expecting to see one.

There is evidence that up to a tenth of the weight of a two-year-old pillow is made up of house dust mites and their droppings. Eeuurrgghh!

▼ BIG BEETLE

The Goliath beetle is one of the longest – and certainly the heaviest – insects in the world. This giant bug is over 12 centimetres (5 inches) long and weighs about as much as an apple. It might look scary, but it's very useful as it eats dead plant material and animal poo.

▲ DRAGONFLIES

In addition to being some of the most beautiful insects around, dragonflies and damselflies are also some of the biggest. These colourful marvels can have wingspans approaching 20 centimetres (8 inches) across. However, compared with their prehistoric ancestors, this is tiny.

Micro

▲ BIG SHELL

The giant African land snail's name is a bit of a giveaway – this huge gastropod is the largest snail in the world and can grow up to 20 centimetres (8 inches) long. You wouldn't want to find one of those crawling over your salad!

▲ TINY, BUT TROUBLE

We've all heard of animals being infected by insects such as fleas, but would you think that insects also get infected? Well, it happens, and sometimes with deadly effect. Honey bees can become infested with a microscopic mite called *Acarapis woodi*. It makes the adult bees unable to fly and they lose their sense of direction. Bees that can't fly can't find food, so the colony begins to die off.

▶ SHARING A BED

You probably haven't seen one of these in real life, but you've certainly slept with one! It's a house dust mite, and you'd need pretty good eyesight to spot it because it is less than 0.02 centimetres (0.008 inches) in length. Still, your bed mattress could well be home to millions of them! These mites eat dead skin, so really they're doing a clean-up job for us.

Contributor credits:
3-D glasses illustrator: Ian Thompson
3-D images by Pinsharp 3-D Graphics

Further credits by chapter:

DINOSAURS
Author: Heather Amery
Picture credits: Ardea London Ltd; Discovery Communications
Inc; Natural History Museum (London).

SNAKES
Author: Paul Harrison
Picture credits: Nature Picture Library; NHPA; Science Photo
Library.

SHARKS
Authors: Lynn Gibbons and Chris Coode
Picture credits: BBC; Planet Earth; Oxford Scientific Films.

REPTILES
Author: Paul Harrison
Picture credits: Nature Picture Library; NHPA; Oxford
Scientific (OSF/Photolibrary.com; Science Photo Library;
John White Photos.

KILLER CATS
Author: Paul Harrison
Picture credits: Ardea London Ltd; Bridgeman Art Library;
Nature Picture Library; NHPA; Oxford Scientific
(OSF/Photolibrary.com); Science Photo Library.

BUGS
Author: Paul Harrison
Picture credits: FLPA; Nature Picture Library; NHPA; Oxford
Scientific (OSF/Photolibrary.com).